EXPLORING OUR SOLAR SYSTEM

MARS

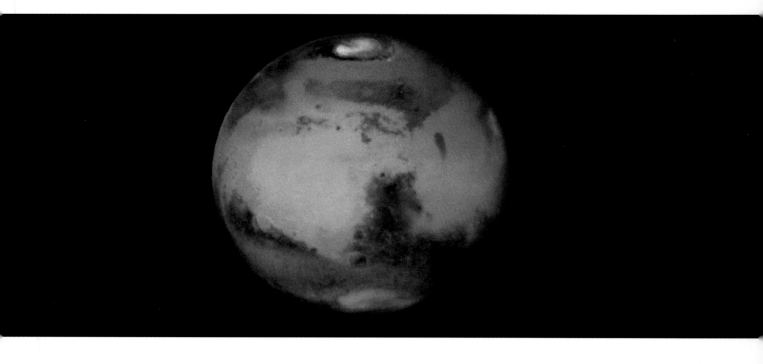

DAVID JEFFERIS

Crabtree

■ ABOUT MARS

Mars is often called the red planet because of its vast plains of rust-red sand. Mars is also known for its deep valleys and huge volcanoes. It is popular in science fiction, with books and movies portraying "Martians" as Earth invaders.

In reality, Earth has invaded Mars, in the form of machines that have explored some of the planet's surface. Mars is still the most likely planet in our solar system to have some sort of life, even if that life is only a few primitive **micro-organisms**. This makes the red planet an exciting target for research.

Crabtree Publishing Company
PMB 16A,
350 Fifth Avenue, Suite 3308
New York, NY 10118

616 Welland Avenue,
St. Catharines, Ontario
L2M 5V6

Editors: Ellen Rodger,
Robert Walker
Adrianna Morganelli

Published by Crabtree Publishing
Company © 2008

Written and produced by:
David Jefferis/Buzz Books

Educational advisor:
Julie Stapleton

Science advisor:
Mat Irvine FBIS

■ ACKNOWLEDGEMENTS
We wish to thank all those people who have helped to create this publication. Information and images were supplied by:

Agencies and organizations:
    Arizona State University/Ron Miller
    ESA European Space Agency
    HST Hubble Space Telescope
    JPL Jet Propulsion Laboratory
    MSSS Malin Space Science Systems
    NASA Space Agency
    NASA/JPL/Brown University
    Pearson Prentice Hall, Inc.
Collections:
    Alpha Archive
    iStockphoto/Julien Grondin

Library and Archives Canada Cataloguing in Publication

Jefferis, David   Mars : distant red planet / David Jefferis.

(Exploring our solar system) Includes index.
ISBN 978-0-7787-3732-2 (bound).--
ISBN 978-0-7787-3748-3 (pbk.)

1. Mars (Planet)--Juvenile literature. I. Title. II. Series:
Exploring our solar system (St. Catharines, Ont.)

QB641.J445 2008   j523.43   C2008-901516-9

Library of Congress Cataloging-in-Publication Data

Jefferis, David.
  Mars : distant red planet / David Jefferis.
      p. cm. -- (Exploring our solar system)
  Includes index.
  ISBN-13: 978-0-7787-3748-3 (pbk. : alk. paper)
  ISBN-10: 0-7787-3748-9 (pbk. : alk. paper)
  ISBN-13: 978-0-7787-3732-2 (reinforced library binding : alk. paper)
  ISBN-10: 0-7787-3732-2 (reinforced library binding : alk. paper)
  1. Mars (Planet)--Juvenile literature. I. Title.
  QB641.J445 2008
  523.43--dc22

                                                    2008008775

CONTENTS

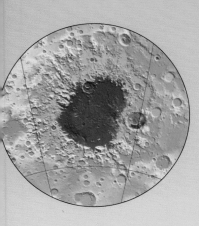

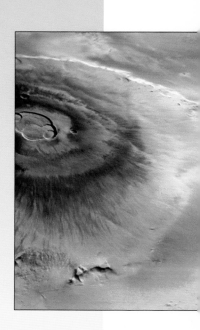

■ WHAT IS THE RED PLANET?

Mars is one of eight major planets that circle around the Sun. It is a sphere that measures 4,220 miles (6,794 km) across.

Moon

Earth

Mars

Phobos and Deimos

■ Here the Moon, Earth, Mars, and its two moons are shown to scale. Mars is much smaller than the Earth, but because it has no seas or oceans, its land area is only a little less than our world.

■ HOW DID MARS GET ITS NAME?

Mars appears as a ruby-red point of light in the night skies of Earth. To the Romans, it looked like blood, so they named it Mars, after their god of war.

WOW! Before the Romans, the Greeks also named the red planet after their god of war. Its name was Ares. Today, the study of Martian geology is called "areology."

■ HOW BIG ARE ITS TWO MOONS?

Compared with our own Moon, the moons of Mars are tiny. Phobos and Deimos are so small that nobody saw them until they were spotted by U.S. astronomer Asaph Hall in 1877. The bigger of the two is potato-shaped Phobos. It is less than 17 miles (27 km) long.

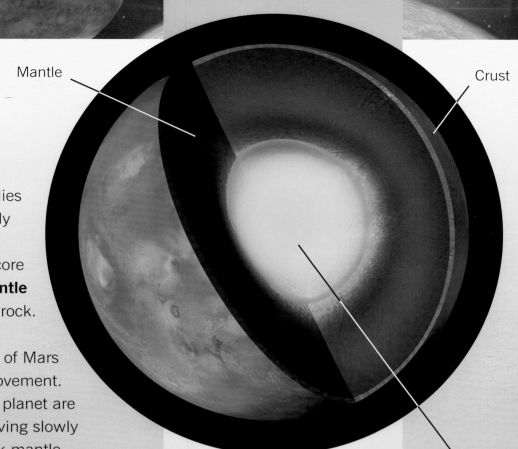

Mantle

Crust

Core

■ IS MARS A SOLID BALL OF ROCK?

We do not yet know what lies deep inside Mars. It is likely that Mars has a solid **core**, made mostly of iron. The core is surrounded by a hot **mantle** and an outer **crust** of cold rock.

Unlike the Earth, the crust of Mars is solid, with no sign of movement. The continents of our own planet are like giant rocky plates, moving slowly as they float on a hot, thick mantle.

■ HOW FAR AWAY IS THE SUN?

Mars is the fourth planet from the Sun, and its average distance is about 142 million miles (229 million km). Earth **orbits** the Sun at the much closer distance of about 93 million miles (150 million km).

■ The rocky crust of Mars is thought to be thicker than that of the Earth. It averages about 31 miles (50 km) thick, instead of the 25 miles (40 km) thickness of the Earth's crust.

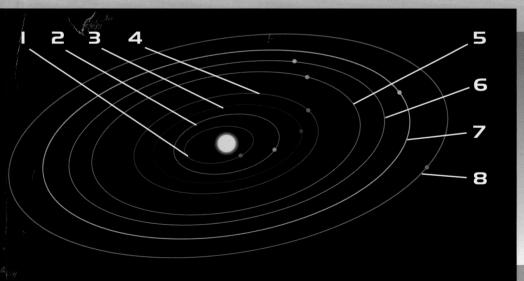

■ Mars is the outermost of the rocky planets. Like the other planets, it follows a curving path around the Sun, called its orbit.

1	Mercury	5	Jupiter
2	Venus	6	Saturn
3	Earth	7	Uranus
4	Mars	8	Neptune

◼ HOW LONG IS A DAY ON MARS?

A day on Mars is called a "sol." It is just over half an hour longer than Earth's 24 hours. It is 24 hours, 39 minutes, and 35 seconds long.

◼ The Sun looks a little smaller from Mars, and temperatures never reach higher than a mild day on Earth. Here, a Mars rover snapped a picture of a Martian sunset.

◼ HOW LONG IS A MARTIAN YEAR?

A year on Mars lasts for 687 Earth days. It is longer than a year o Earth, because Mars is further from the Sun, so it has a greater distance to travel in its orbital path around the Sun. It also travels slower through space, at 15 miles per second (24 km/sec), compared to Earth's 18.5 miles per second (30 km/sec).

◼ HOW HEAVY WOULD I BE ON MARS?

Mars is smaller than Earth, and has weaker **gravity**. On Mars, you would be just one-third of your Earth weight.

◼ The low gravity of Mars provides amazing sights. For example, carbon dioxide gas geysers **erupt near the Martian poles, blasting dust and dirt far higher than they could on Earth.**

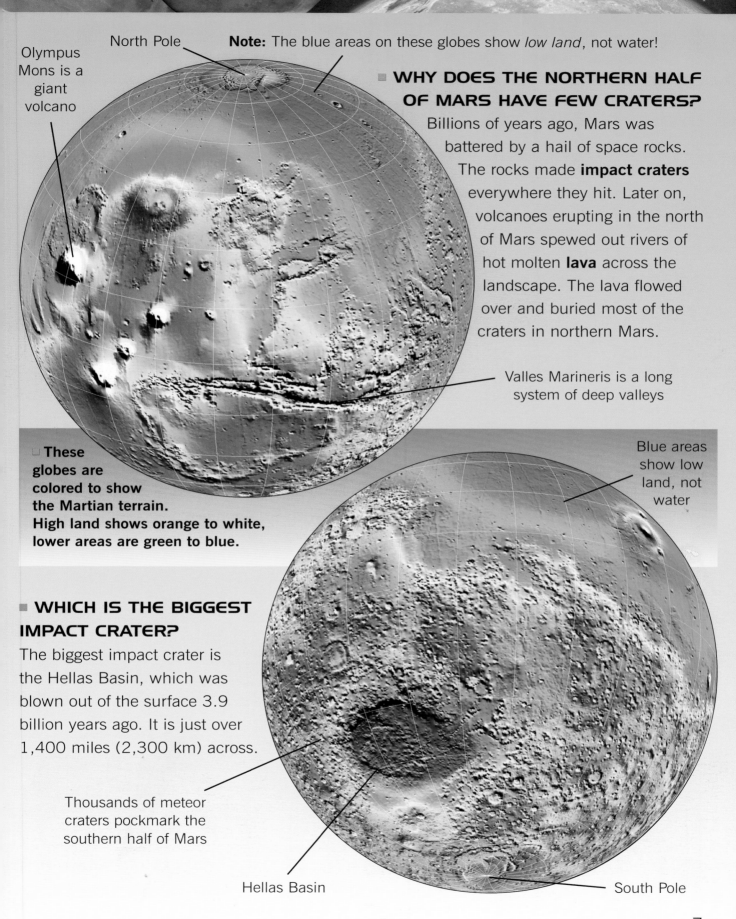

Olympus Mons is a giant volcano

North Pole

Note: The blue areas on these globes show *low land*, not water!

WHY DOES THE NORTHERN HALF OF MARS HAVE FEW CRATERS?

Billions of years ago, Mars was battered by a hail of space rocks. The rocks made **impact craters** everywhere they hit. Later on, volcanoes erupting in the north of Mars spewed out rivers of hot molten **lava** across the landscape. The lava flowed over and buried most of the craters in northern Mars.

Valles Marineris is a long system of deep valleys

☐ **These globes are colored to show the Martian terrain. High land shows orange to white, lower areas are green to blue.**

Blue areas show low land, not water

WHICH IS THE BIGGEST IMPACT CRATER?

The biggest impact crater is the Hellas Basin, which was blown out of the surface 3.9 billion years ago. It is just over 1,400 miles (2,300 km) across.

Thousands of meteor craters pockmark the southern half of Mars

Hellas Basin

South Pole

■ HAVE ROBOTS EXPLORED MARS?

Dozens of missions have been launched to Mars.
Among the biggest successes have been the U.S. surface rovers.

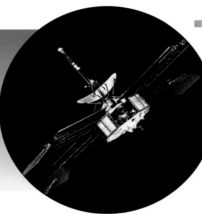

■ Mariner 4 was a 575 lb (261 kg) probe, equipped with a TV camera and other instruments. Mariner returned 21 pictures to Earth before flying on into deep space.

■ WHAT DID THE FIRST SPACE PROBES FIND OUT?

The U.S. Mariner 4 of 1964-1965 was the first successful space probe to Mars. It did not land, but did take pictures as it flew past. Scientists were disappointed when, instead of a world with life on it, Mars seemed to be a dusty, dead planet.

■ HOW DID VIKING LANDERS TEST THE MARTIAN SOIL?

The first robots on Mars were two U.S. Viking landers that touched down on different parts of the planet in 1976. They did not move around on wheels, but each had cameras, and a long arm that dug out soil samples.

Viking 2's landing site was a rocky plain

■ The Vikings each had a small laboratory. The lab automatically checked the soil samples for any signs of Martian life.

Life-size Viking display model

WOW!
Scientists were worried that the Viking probes might take Earth micro-organisms to Mars. Before flight, both Vikings were "cooked" or heat-treated to kill "bugs."

■ HOW DOES A ROBOT EXPLORER LAND SAFELY ON THE RED PLANET?

Making the journey to Mars is difficult enough, and making a safe landing even more so. Equipment has to be in working order after touchdown. The solution for a safe landing, first used by the Mars Pathfinder mission of 1997, was to use airbags. Airbags cushioned the landing for the rover, called Sojourner. Like the airbags used in road vehicles to protect people in a crash, a "ball of bags" inflated before landing, then bounced and rolled to a standstill.

■ These pictures show how the Spirit and Opportunity rovers of 2004, arrived on Mars.

1 Lander leaves its carrier rocket.

2 Lander enters the atmosphere inside a protective heatshield.

3 A parachute slows the Lander, rockets brake it more, airbags inflate to protect rover.

4 Airbag ball drops to the ground.

5 The airbags deflate, and the rover crawls out slowly and safely.

■ Sojourner was the first Mars rover. Here it checks out a rock named Yogi.

■ WHAT EXPLORING TOOLS DO ROVERS CARRY?

Every space mission is different, but the two rovers Spirit and Opportunity that landed on Mars in 2004, had similar equipment. Cameras are used for guidance and photography. A RAT (Rock Abrasion Tool) grinds rocks to see what they are made of. Magnets collect magnetic dust particles. An MI (Microscopic Imager) is used to make extremely close observations.

■WHY IS MARS CALLED THE RED PLANET?

Mars is called the red planet because from Earth it looks like a red ball. This color matches the reality of the planet's surface conditions.

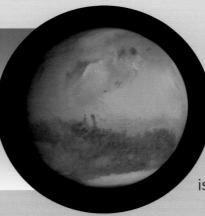

■ This is about the best view of Mars you can see in a telescope. Light and dark areas were once thought to be land and seas. We now know that Mars is a dry planet.

■ WHAT CAUSES THE COLOR?

Mars is a reddish-brown shade because much of its surface is covered with iron-rich soil. This soil reacts with the small amounts of oxygen in the Martian air. The result of this chemical reaction is a planet-wide powder coating of rust!

WOW!

We know quite a lot about Mars rocks because volcanoes blew many of them into space million of years ago. Many have since fallen to Earth as meteors.

■ WHAT ELSE IS IN THE SOIL?

The surface rocks of Mars seem to be made mostly of **basalt**. On Earth, basalt is a common gray-black volcanic rock. On Mars, it is a giveaway to the planet's violent past, when hundreds of huge volcanoes erupted millions of years ago to form much of the surface we see today.

■ This crater was formed by an ancient meteor impact. Other craters on Mars were made by erupting volcanoes.

■ WHAT IS IN THE LANDSCAPE?

The views are mostly of rocks and more rocks, stretching to the horizon. Many scenes are dramatic. The picture below is a view of the half-mile (800 m) wide Victoria crater. You can see the ripples of sand dunes in the bottom, while on the left, it is overlooked by a 50 ft (15m) high cliff.

■ The Ares Vallis is a valley that could have been formed by fluid – possibly water – in the distant past. It was photographed by the U.S. Mars Pathfinder space probe in 1997.

■ WHAT TOOK THE PHOTO BELOW?

It was taken in 2006, by the U.S. robot surveyor Opportunity. Several pictures were taken, then joined to make this wide shot.

Opportunity rover

IS MARS A DUSTY PLANET?

It certainly is! Mars is a desert planet and dust plays a big part in conditions there, both on the surface and in the air.

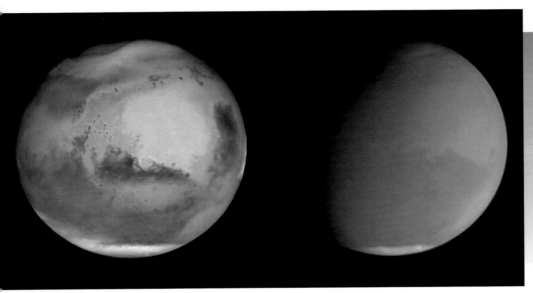

☐ **Dust storms on Mars can be HUGE! The picture (left) was taken in June 2001, and shows surface features through clear skies.**

Shortly after this picture was taken, a dust storm blew up and soon covered the planet (right). In September, the whole of Mars was a dusty blur.

■ WHEN DID WE FIRST SEE A MARTIAN DUST STORM?

We found out about these storms in 1971, when the U.S. Mariner 9 space probe arrived near Mars. Instead of sharp pictures of the surface, scientists were surprised to see nothing but fuzzy pictures of a planet-wide dust storm. Now we know that such storms happen often on the red planet.

■ ARE DUST STORMS ELECTRIC?

The storms create **static electricity** as dust grains rub against each other. It is the same effect you get when you rub a balloon against your sweater. The static is powerful enough to create bolts of lightning in the bigger dust storms (left).

WOW!
Dust stays high in the Martian air for weeks, mostly because it is so dry. On Earth, dust is usually rained out of the sky after only a few hours.

Clean solar panels   Dusty solar panels

■ The Spirit rover shows how dust collects everywhere. The solar panels were clean to start with (left). After nearly two Mars years they were covered in dust (right). High winds later blew some of the dust off.

■ ARE DUST STORMS DANGEROUS?

Gritty Mars dust certainly interferes with machinery. In 2007, the rovers Spirit and Opportunity got covered with dust. The rovers started to run very low on power because dust covered their **solar panels**, which generate electricity from sunlight. In fact, much of the science equipment onboard the rovers had to be shut down until the storms cleared.

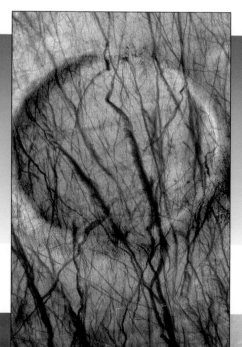

■ The strange stripes across a crater in this image were a mystery until a photograph taken by the Spirit rover uncovered the cause (right).
   The stripes were caused by a dust devil, **one of the many small whirlwinds that spin across the dusty Mars landscape.**

13 ■

■COULD I BREATHE ON MARS?

The atmosphere on Mars is very thin. It is made mostly of carbon dioxide, a gas that humans cannot breathe safely.

■ WHAT ELSE IS IN THE MARTIAN AIR?

The atmosphere of Mars is very different to that of the Earth. It consists of 95 percent carbon dioxide, 3 percent nitrogen, 1.6 percent argon, with traces of oxygen, water, and methane. The Martian air is quite dusty, which gives it a pale brownish-pink color, instead of the intense blue of the skies of Earth.

◻ **This picture, taken by a space probe in orbit around Mars, clearly shows the brownish tint of the atmosphere, outlined between the horizon and the pitch black of space above.**

■ HOW THIN IS THE ATMOSPHERE?

The Martian air is very thin. At ground level, it is about 30 times thinner than the air at the top of Mount Everest, the Earth's highest mountain. In winter, temperatures get so cold that up to a quarter of the atmosphere freezes to form carbon dioxide snow and ice that falls in polar regions.

■ **Mars has seasons, like the Earth. They are much longer than Earth's seasons, because on Mars, one year lasts for 687 days. A winter's day on Mars would freeze you solid in just a few minutes.**

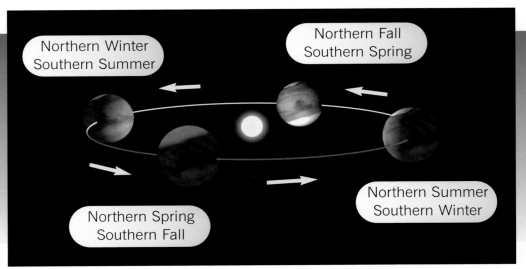

Northern Winter
Southern Summer

Northern Fall
Southern Spring

Northern Spring
Southern Fall

Northern Summer
Southern Winter

■ WHAT ARE THE CLOUDS OF MARS MADE FROM?

The misty white patches on this picture are very high clouds, which can be up to 62 miles (100 km) above the surface of Mars. They are made of carbon dioxide or water-ice particles. They usually form around fine dust blown into the air during big storms.

■ The clouds show up well in this picture because they are reflecting the Sun's rays.

If you could stand on the surface of Mars and look up, you would see these clouds as little more than wispy streaks, high in the sky.

15

WHAT IS THE BIGGEST VOLCANO ON MARS?

Olympus Mons, on the surface of the planet, is the biggest known volcano in the solar system.

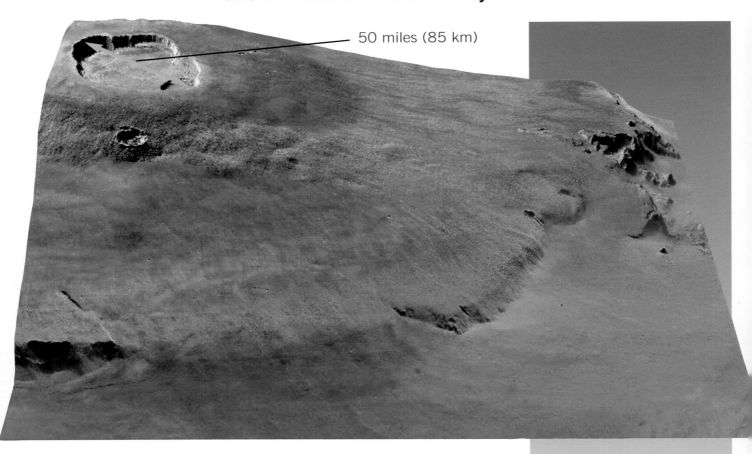

50 miles (85 km)

HOW HIGH IS OLYMPUS MONS?

The mighty volcano rises 16.7 miles (27 km) above the surrounding Martian plains. Compared to this, Earth's highest volcano, Mauna Kea in the Pacific Ocean, is only a foothill, at just 6.06 miles (9.75 km) high.

View of Olympus Mons from Mars orbit

This computer image is specially colored to show details on the slopes of Olympus Mons.

There are several linked craters, or calderas, at the top. These were probably formed when the ground collapsed after the volcano stopped erupting.

■ WHAT KIND OF VOLCANO IS OLYMPUS MONS?

It is called a **shield volcano**. Shield volcanoes slowly build up into a wide mountain when fluid lava pours out over a long period of time. The lava cools to form rock. Over millions of years, Olympus Mons grew steadily bigger. It probably stopped being active many millions of years ago, but there may still be some small eruptions.

□ Some Martian volcanoes seem to have no caldera. This one, called Terra Cimmeria, has a flat top. In fact, the caldera is still there, but it has been filled by drifting sand. This happened a long time ago, as there are some smaller craters, caused by more recent meteor impacts.

■ ARE THERE OTHER VOLCANOES ON MARS?

Yes, there are plenty of them, although none are as big as Olympus Mons. Three shield volcanoes called Ascraeus, Pavonis, and Arsia Mons are smaller than Olympus Mons, but because they lie on high ground their summits are nearly as tall. Thin, white clouds often swirl around their summits.

□ Millions of years ago, a Martian volcano could have looked like this, as it spewed rivers of scorching-hot lava across the landscape. The bubbling mass spread out, to eventually form a huge plain of cooled lava.

■HOW DEEP ARE MARTIAN VALLEYS?

The deepest valley on Mars is the enormous Valles Marineris. It is a huge system of canyons bigger than anything like it on Earth.

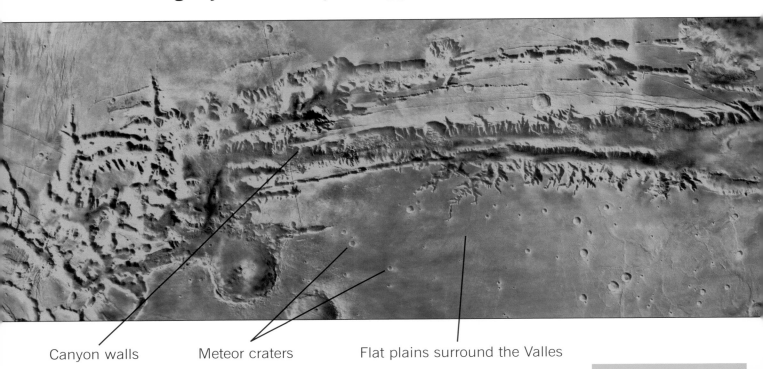

Canyon walls

Meteor craters

Flat plains surround the Valles

■ HOW BIG IS VALLES MARINERIS?

It is a complex system of valleys and chasms that winds its way across the Martian landscape for more than 2,500 miles (4,000 km). This is about the same width as the United States.

WOW!
Parts of the Valles may have been blasted away by underground pockets of carbon dioxide. These could have blasted soil and rocks away like super powerful "gas guns."

■ AND HOW DEEP IS IT?

The deepest parts of Valles Marineris plunge to more than 4 miles (7 km) below the surrounding plains. If there is life on Mars, the valley bottoms may be a good place to look.

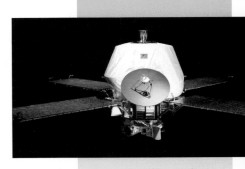

■ **Valles Marineris is named after the U.S. Mariner 9 space probe that first took photos of it in 1972.**

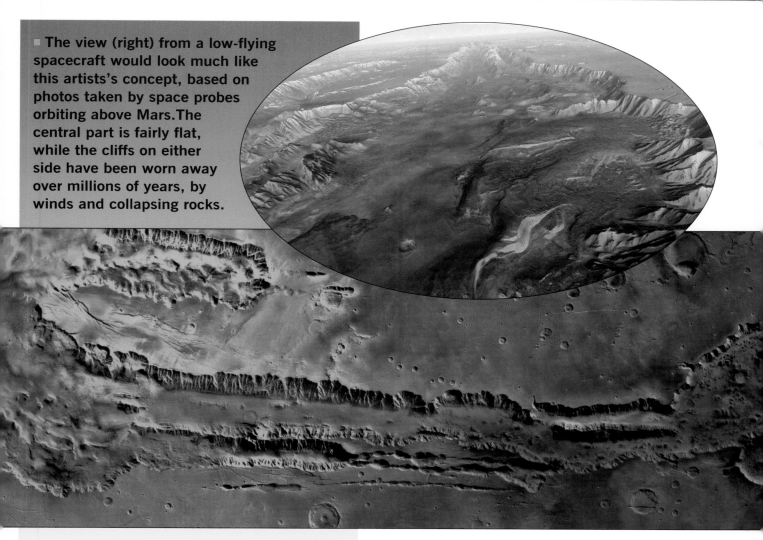

■ The view (right) from a low-flying spacecraft would look much like this artists's concept, based on photos taken by space probes orbiting above Mars. The central part is fairly flat, while the cliffs on either side have been worn away over millions of years, by winds and collapsing rocks.

■ WHAT CAUSED THE VALLES?

It is thought that much of the Valles is a **rift valley**, with part of the crust slumping down into the mantle below. The most similar feature on Earth is the African Rift Valley, but it is not as wide or as deep as the Valles.

■ ARE THERE ANY RIVERS THERE?

Not at present, because water can only exist briefly as a liquid on Mars. It turns to vapor very quickly in the thin air. It is believed that some river-like channels may have been carved by water in the distant past.

□ One day it may be possible for astronauts to explore the Valles area.

It is a job that should be made a little less dangerous by the light gravity of Mars. Using ropes and other types of climbing gear will be much easier.

■ARE THE POLES ICY?

Mars is further from the Sun than the Earth, and its winters are twice as long. The Martian poles are far colder than anywhere on Earth.

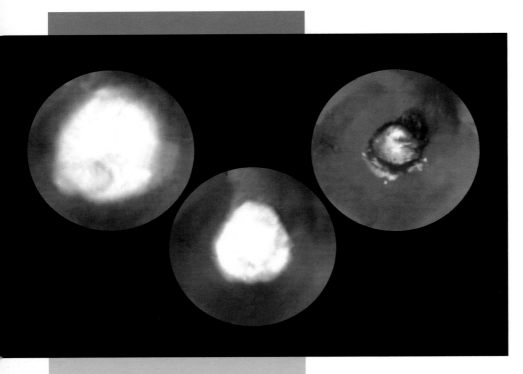

■ HOW COLD IS A MARTIAN WINTER?

Temperatures at the Martian poles make Earth's polar regions seem almost inviting. On Mars, temperatures drop to about -220°F (-140°C) in winter, compared with the Earth's record of -128.6°F (-89.2°C). The south polar region is more extreme than the north, because Mars is further from the Sun during southern winters.

■ These pictures show six months in the life of the northern ice cap of Mars. In mid-winter, the ice cap has grown to its biggest size, but as the Sun's rays warm it up in springtime, the ice starts to melt. A few months later, the ice cap has shrunk even more.

■ HOW BIG ARE THE ICE CAPS?

The northern ice cap is about 745 miles (1,200 km) across in winter. The colder southern ice cap is only one-third of this, but has much deeper ice.

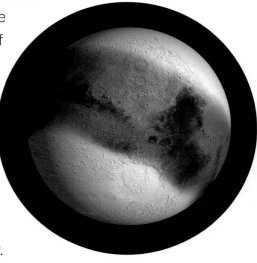

■ DOES MARS HAVE ICE AGES?

Research suggests that Mars may have had an ice age as recently as 400,000 years ago. If so, Mars may have looked like a striped ball (right), with ice reaching almost to the equator.

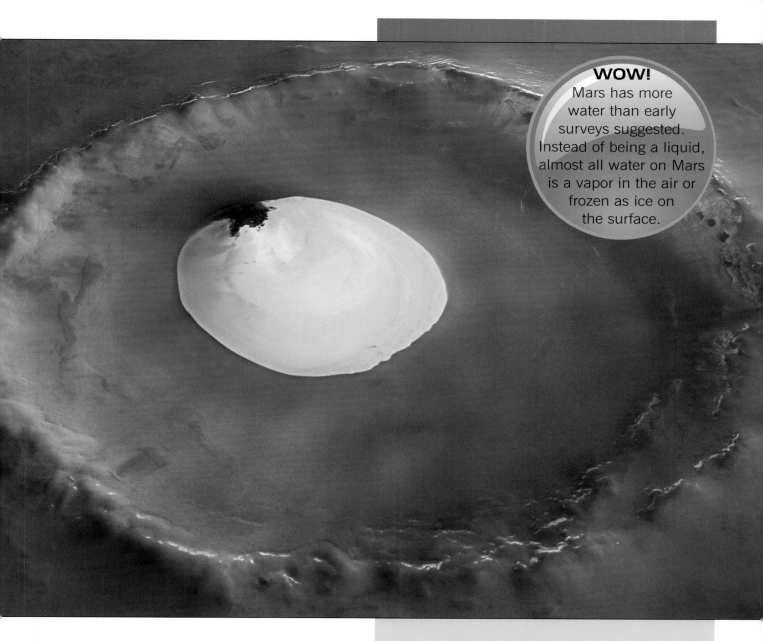

WOW!
Mars has more water than early surveys suggested. Instead of being a liquid, almost all water on Mars is a vapor in the air or frozen as ice on the surface.

■ IS THERE WATER AT THE POLES?

The polar ice caps are made almost entirely of frozen water that is up to 1.8 miles (3 km) deep. There is enough water in the southern ice cap alone to cover the whole planet to a depth of 36 ft (11 m). Frozen carbon dioxide, or "**dry ice**," covers the northern ice cap in winter, but it mostly disappears as vapor into the atmosphere in summer. The smaller but colder southern ice cap has permanent dry ice cover 26 ft (8 m) deep.

■ This picture was taken by the orbiting Mars Express space probe in 2005. It shows an impact crater not far from the Martian North Pole, with a big drift of water-ice in it. The crater is some 22 miles (35 km) across, so that makes the ice as big as a small city here on Earth. Ice has also formed on the shadowed crater walls, at right.

HOW BIG ARE THE MOONS OF MARS?

The two moons of Mars are very small. Even the bigger moon, Phobos, is less than 17 miles (27 km) long.

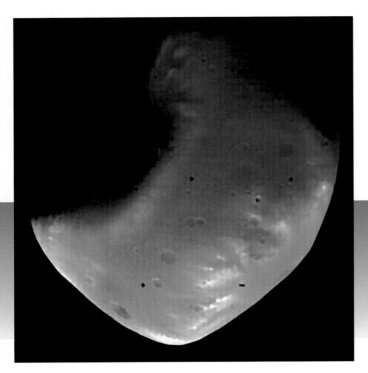

■ WHAT DO THEIR NAMES MEAN?

Most astronomical objects are named after names or places mentioned in the myths of ancient Rome or Greece. The two moons of Mars were named after the sons of Ares, the Greek god of war. Phobos means "fear," and Deimos means "panic."

■ Deimos (left) is a chunk of rock just 9.3 miles (15 km) long. Its gravity is so low that you could leave it just by jumping off!

■ Phobos (right) is 16.6 miles (26.8 km) long. Its biggest crater (arrowed) is called Stickney, and is 5.6 miles (9 km) across.

■ WHERE DID THE TWO MOONS COME FROM?

The most likely theory is that Phobos and Deimos are chunks of drifting space rock that were drawn to Mars by its gravity. They probably came from the space zone between Mars and the giant planet Jupiter, but we do not know for sure. They could have come from much further away, in the dark, chilly reaches of the outer solar system.

■ At times, the two moons go between the Sun and Mars. Here Phobos is shown crossing the Sun's face.

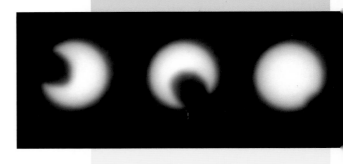

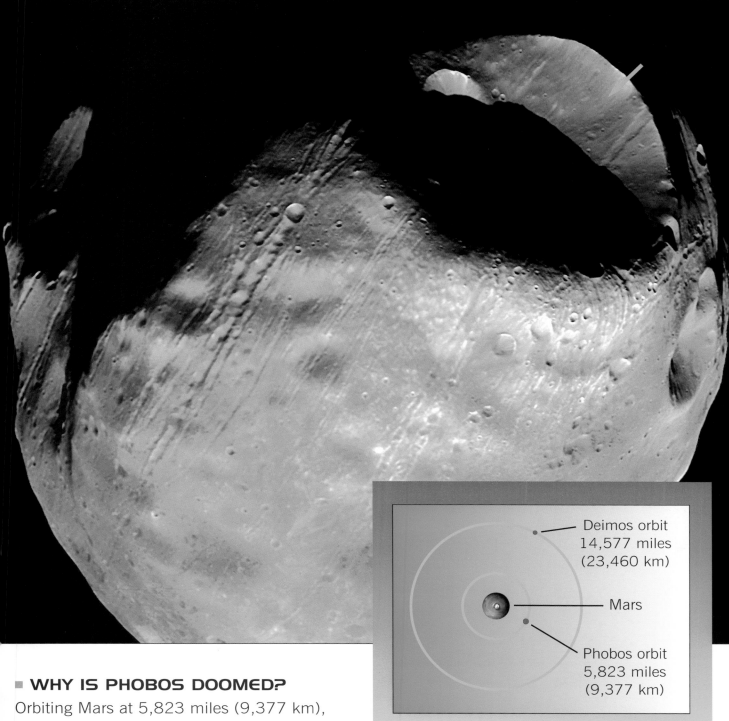

■ WHY IS PHOBOS DOOMED?

Orbiting Mars at 5,823 miles (9,377 km), Phobos is perilously close to breaking up, due to gravity forces tugging at it. The latest research shows that Phobos has only 50 million years or so before it either crashes onto the Martian desert, or shatters into pieces to form a rocky ring around Mars.

Deimos orbit
14,577 miles
(23,460 km)

Mars

Phobos orbit
5,823 miles
(9,377 km)

■ **Phobos has an unusual orbit — it is closer to its planet than any other moon in the solar system. Our Moon is about 249,000 miles (400,000 km) away. Phobos moves so fast that it completes an orbit every eight hours, so there are two moonrises every Martian day!**

IS THERE LIFE ON MARS?

The hunt for some form of alien life has been going on for many years. It is still a red-hot research topic for space scientists.

WHO FIRST THOUGHT THERE MIGHT BE MARTIANS?

The idea dates back to a map of Mars, drawn by the Italian astronomer Giovanni Schiaparelli, in 1877. On the map, he drew various straight lines, which he called "canali," or channels.

In 1895, U.S. astronomer Percival Lowell published a book in which he suggested that Schiaparelli's channels were canals, perhaps built by intelligent lifeforms. Lowell further developed his theory and said the canals were made to take water from the poles to the rest of Mars, so there would be water in the planet's deserts.

■ Percival Lowell was a respected astronomer, and produced several books about Mars. He sketched maps that showed an immense canal system (above). The canals were later proved to be only an optical illusion.

HAVE WE FOUND EVEN A FEW MICRO-ORGANISMS?

For a few weeks in 1996, scientists thought they had found signs of life, buried in a lump of rock that had been blown across space by a volcanic explosion on Mars, millions of years ago. But there was no real proof.

■ These rod-like shapes were briefly thought to be signs of life, found inside a meteor from Mars. The space rock was found in Antarctica, where it had laid untouched on the ice for many years. Eventually, scientists decided that the tiny rods – visible only through a microscope – had really been formed by some chemical reaction in the rock.

■ WHERE COULD WE FIND LIFE?

It is unlikely that there is anything living on the surface of Mars. Conditions there are too harsh. There are plans to dig under the surface to determine if, like Earth, there are micro-organisms living underground.

■ The Phoenix lander was built to see what conditions are like in polar regions. Solar panel fold out to supply electricity for equipment. This includes a robot arm that can dig a hole 1.6 ft (0.5 m) deep. This depth is thought to be roughly where the ice meets soil underneath, and so could be a likely spot to find living things.

■ WHAT IF MARS HAD SEAS?

There is enough ice at the poles to make a shallow sea (left) if it all melted. Scientists think Mars may have had big watery areas in the past. Finding fossils of strange-looking Martian fish is not likely. Prehistoric seas were probably too salty and acidic for such life to develop in the first place.

WOW!
People once thought that Martians were real. In 1938, a radio play had many listeners convinced that invaders from Mars were taking over the Earth!

■HOW CAN I OBSERVE MARS?

Mars is the closest planet to Earth. Despite this, it is still far enough away that to the unaided eye, it never looks bigger than a bright red star.

■ CAN I USE A TELESCOPE?

This is the traditional way to planet-spot, and it is still very satisfying to go out at night and see a space object. Star gazers need a fairly powerful telescope to see Mars.

■ WHAT DOES MARS LOOK LIKE?

The telescope we used for the pictures above was a six-inch reflector (right). It is important to realize that Mars never comes closer to Earth than 35 million miles (56 million km), so even these fuzzy little images are about as good as you are likely to see.

WOW!
Mars and the Earth circle the Sun in different orbits, so the distance between them changes constantly. They pass at their closest approach every 26 months.

■ ARE THERE MAPS OF MARS I CAN BUY?

Most of the basic information you need is freely available on the Internet. A globe like the one shown (right) can give you a better "feel" for the planet than any flat computer image.

■ A six-inch telescope like this is about the minimum you need to get good results for a distant object like Mars. Just as important as the telescope is a very solid tripod to support it.

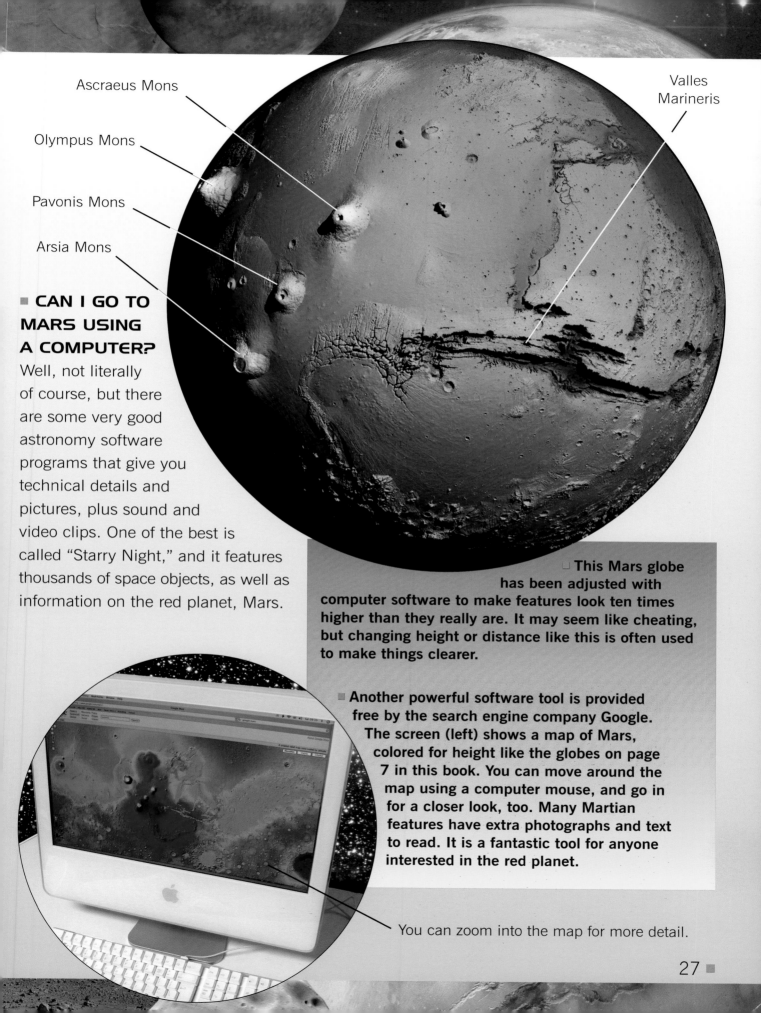

Ascraeus Mons

Olympus Mons

Pavonis Mons

Arsia Mons

Valles
Marineris

■ CAN I GO TO MARS USING A COMPUTER?

Well, not literally of course, but there are some very good astronomy software programs that give you technical details and pictures, plus sound and video clips. One of the best is called "Starry Night," and it features thousands of space objects, as well as information on the red planet, Mars.

□ **This Mars globe has been adjusted with computer software to make features look ten times higher than they really are. It may seem like cheating, but changing height or distance like this is often used to make things clearer.**

■ **Another powerful software tool is provided free by the search engine company Google. The screen (left) shows a map of Mars, colored for height like the globes on page 7 in this book. You can move around the map using a computer mouse, and go in for a closer look, too. Many Martian features have extra photographs and text to read. It is a fantastic tool for anyone interested in the red planet.**

You can zoom into the map for more detail.

■ FACTS AND FIGURES

■ MARS STATISTICS

Diameter

4,220 miles (6,794 km), making Mars just over one-half as wide as the Earth.

Time to rotate

A Martian day (called a sol) lasts for 24 hours, 39 minutes, and 35 seconds.

Distance to the Sun

142 million miles (229 million km) average. The orbit of Mars is not circular, so the distance varies by 25 million miles (40 million km).

Composition

Mars soil is made up mostly of volcanic rock (basalt). Most of the surface is covered with iron-rich dust.

Temperature

The surface temperature on Mars varies across the planet, from the equator to the poles. The average temperature is about -49°F (-45°C). It is much colder at night or in winter. The highest known summer temperature is 68°F (20°C).

Mass

Mars has a mass of just 10 percent that of the Earth.

Surface gravity

Here on Earth we live under a force of one gravity, or 1G. The smaller and less dense Mars has a surface gravity of about one-third that of the Earth.

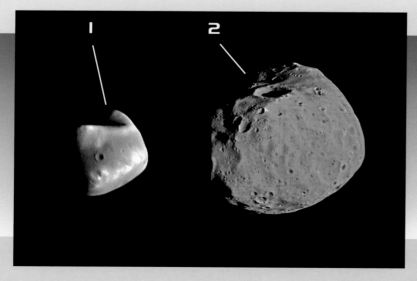

□ The Martian moons Deimos (1) and Phobos (2) are like oversized space boulders, captured by the gravity of Mars. If you were standing on Mars, you would see Phobos rising in the west every 11 hours. The more distant Deimos rises slowly in the east every 2.7 days.

■ This was one of the best pictures taken by the Mars Pathfinder mission. The white shapes in the bottom are parts of the Pathfinder lander, including the airbags used to cushion the landing.

The Sojourner rover was about the size of a microwave oven and at launch, weighed just 25.4 lb (11.5 kg). On Mars, of course, it weighed only one-third of this. Here the rover (arrowed) leaves wheel tracks in the soil as it explores the landing zone.

WHAT IS THE "MARS CURSE"?

It is not a real curse, but a nickname for the sheer difficulty of sending spacecraft all the way to the red planet. About two-thirds of all missions to Mars have ended in failure for one reason or another.

WHAT WAS THE PATHFINDER?

Pathfinder was the successful U.S. Mars mission of 1996-1997. It was the first to land a wheeled rover safely on the surface.

Pathfinder came in two parts: a lander, and a small rover, called Sojourner. Sojourner studied the area around the landing zone for 83 sols. Contact was lost after this, probably because the lander's power supply failed. Without power to send a strong radio signal to Earth, Sojourner went silent.

WERE LATER ROVER MISSIONS ALSO SUCCESSFUL?

Following Pathfinder were the twin rovers of the MER (Mars Exploration Rover) mission.

The rovers MER-A (Spirit) and MER-B (Opportunity) landed on different parts of Mars in January 2004. They were designed to last just 90 sols but kept going in amazingly good condition for years after this.

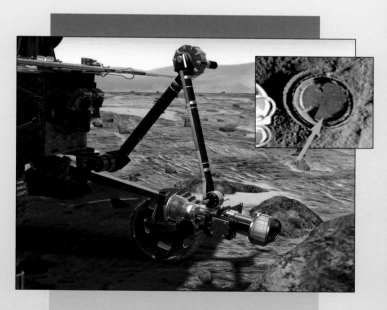

■ Spirit and Opportunity both carried a RAT (Rock Abrasion Tool). This was a rotary grinder, attached to a robot arm. With it, the rovers could drill a shallow hole (arrowed) to see inside various rocks and find out what they were made of.

■ GLOSSARY

Here are explanations for many of the terms used in this book.

Alien A general name for life that may be found one day, beyond Earth.

Basalt A dark, fine-grained volcanic rock that covers much of the northern plains of Mars.

■ **Impact craters cover much of southern Mars. This is Maunder Crater. It is just over 66 miles (107 km) across.**

Caldera A large volcanic crater, usually formed when the top of a volcano collapses after an eruption.

Carbon dioxide A colorless gas that makes up most of the atmosphere of Mars. On Earth, carbon dioxide is expelled by humans and animals as they breathe, and absorbed by plants.

Core The center of a planet. The core of Mars is thought to be made of hot, molten iron, with some sulphur.

Crust The outermost layer of a rocky planet such as Mars.

Dry ice Frozen carbon dioxide.

Dust devil A small whirlwind made of spinning dust and air.

Geyser On Mars, a jet of carbon dioxide gas that squirts into the air.

Gravity The universal force of attraction between all objects.

Impact crater A crater formed by a meteor hitting the ground. Mars has 45,000 impact craters that are more than 3 miles (5 km) across.

Lava Molten rock spewed out from a volcano. Lava is so hot that it flows as a fiery liquid.

Mantle The part of Mars that lies between the crust and the core.

Mass The amount of matter that an object contains.

Meteor A lump of rock drifting in space. When a meteor hits Earth, it is then called a meteorite.

■ **Part of the Mars rift valley, Valles Marineris. It is the biggest of its kind that humans have found so far.**

Part of the Sun to the same scale as the planets

1 2 3 4   5   6   7 8

Micro-organism A living thing so small that it can be seen only through a microscope.

Orbit The curving path a space object takes around a more massive one, such as Mars orbiting the Sun.

Rift valley A long depression caused by a section of ground slumping down, leaving steep side walls.

Shield volcano A broad, domed volcano with gently sloping sides. It is caused by a steady spread of lava over many years.

Solar panel A flat panel that changes the energy in sunlight to electricity.

Solar system The name for the Sun and the various space objects that circle it in their orbits These include the eight major planets, dwarf planets, moons, plus billions of rocks, and space dust.

Static electricity Electricity caused by friction, causing sparks, crackling, and attraction of dust or hair. On Mars, dust storms are thought to be filled with static, caused by dust particles rubbing together.

■ Here are the Sun and major planets:
1 Mercury
2 Venus
3 Earth
4 Mars
5 Jupiter
6 Saturn
7 Uranus
8 Neptune

■ **GOING FURTHER**

Using the Internet is a great way to expand your knowledge of the red planet.

Your first visit should be to the site of the U.S. space agency, NASA. Its site shows almost everything to do with space, from the history of spaceflight to astronomy, and also plans for future Mars missions.

There are also other websites that give detailed space information. Try these sites to start with:

http://www.nasa.gov	A huge site.
http://www.space.com/mars	Lots of general info.
http://www.google.com/mars	Zoom in up close!
http://www.starrynightstore.com	Good software.
http://www.spacedaily.com	Ace for space news.

■ INDEX

Printed in the U.S.A.